Feb 2018

P9-DUT-900

IT'LL NEVER WORK
IN THE
HOME

JON RICHARDS

W
FRANKLIN WATTS
LONDON•SYDNEY

Franklin Watts
First published in Great Britain in 2016 by
The Watts Publishing Group
Copyright © The Watts Publishing
Group, 2016

All rights reserved.

Credits
Conceived, designed and edited by
Tall Tree Ltd
Series Editor: David John
Series Designer: Gary Hyde

Every attempt has been made to clear copyright.
Should there be any inadvertent omission please
apply to the publisher for rectification.

ISBN 978 1 4451 5031 4

Printed in China

Franklin Watts
An imprint of
Hachette Children's Group
Part of The Watts Publishing Group
Carmelite House
50 Victoria Embankment
London EC4Y 0DZ

An Hachette UK Company
www.hachette.co.uk

www.franklinwatts.co.uk

Picture credits:
t-top, b-bottom, l-left, r-right,
c-centre, m-middle
All images public domain unless otherwise
indicated:
Front cover cl, 2, 9bl dreamstime.com/Denis Linine, mcr
Fletcher6 cc Attribution-Share Alike, bl dreamstime.com/
Draftmode, bcl dreamstime.com/Hemul, br, 22br dreamstime.
com/Anskuw, back cover tl, 3t, 29tl dreamstime.com/Hannu
Viitanen, tr, 29bl dreamstime.com/Haiyin, cr dreamstime.com/
Natalya Aksenova, 1, 17t courtesy Library of Congress, 3br, 17cr
istockphoto.com/s-cphoto, 4c dreamstime.com/Ian Keirle, 4b
Nessy-Pic cc Attribution-Share Alike, 5tr dreamstime.com/
Martin Brayley, 5cr dreamstime.com/trekandshoot, 5b
dreamstime.com/Alexandre Zveiger, 6cr dreamstime.com/
Fernando Madeira, 7t dreamstime.com/Oleksandr Delyk, 7b
dreamstime.com/Lio2012, 8cr dreamstime.com/Andrey Maslakov,
9tl courtesy of NARA, 10cl dreamstime.com/Chelovek, 10br
courtesy of Library of Congress, 11br Granger, NYC./Alamy Stock
Photo, 12 bl dreamstime.com/Serghei Starus, 13t Erik Burton cc
Attribution-Share Alike, 14bl dreamstime.com/Foto21293, 15t
dreamstime.com/Vldimir Talmudic, 15bl courtesy of NASA, 16cr
Ferdinand Reus cc Attribution-Share Alike, 17bl dreamstime.com/
Martin Kawalski, 18tl dreamstime.com/Gioncla, 18br SSPL/Getty
Images, 19b dreamstime.com/Danielmenr, 20bcl dreamstime.com/
Sergei Kazakov, 21b dreamstime.com/Brad Calkins, 22cl
dreamstime.com/Marcin Chodorowski, 23cl dreamstime.com/
Jack309, 23br dreamstime.com/Chutima Chaochaiya, 24cl Musik-
och teatermuseet cc Attribution-Share Alike, 24br dreamstime.
com/Wisconsinart, 25bl dreamstime.com/Imtmphoto, 26br
dreamstime.com/Bagwold, 27br dreamstime.com/Hse0193, 28cr
courtesy of Library of Congress, 28bl dreamstime.com/Everett
Collection Inc.

CONTENTS

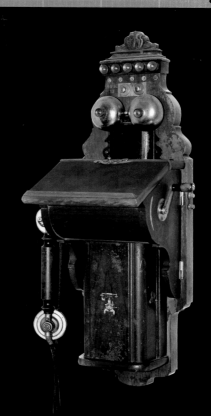

HOMES OVER THE YEARS

Throughout the ages, the homes we live in have been shaped by the technology and materials of the period. Thousands of years ago, homes were simple shelters. Today's homes are multi-roomed and gadget-packed.

Iron Age roofs were made of straw. There were no chimneys.

IRON AGE HOUSE

The Iron Age began in about 1200 BCE and lasted for more than a thousand years. Iron Age homes had a single room that was used for eating and sleeping. People shared the room with livestock, such as sheep and chickens. At the centre was an open fire for heating and cooking, with simple seating made from logs. People slept on straw and used wool clothing and furs to keep warm.

The floor was made from packed earth.

A ROOM FOR EVERYONE? 👉

For hundreds of years until the 1600s, most homes had timber frames and clay walls, with thatched straw for a roof. After the 1600s, more homes were built of brick, which was safer than timber as it did not catch fire so easily. Poor people often lived together in one room and shared a toilet with other families. The rich had rooms for servants who cooked and cleaned.

These houses from the 1500s in Rye, UK, are a mix of timber and brick.

MODERN HOME 👉

Today, modern homes may be built of steel frames, and clad in concrete, brick or stone. They are full of technology. Central heating systems heat every part of the house in winter, and air-conditioning keeps it cool in summer. Digital technology keeps us entertained with widescreen TVs, while superfast Internet sends information, music and movies to laptops, tablets and smartphones.

Where land is scarce and expensive, homes are stacked in towers of apartments.

A modern home has central heating, wi-fi and energy-saving lighting.

KEEPING WARM

Our homes protect us from the weather when it's cold outside. A century ago, homes were still heated by fires. Today, homes use clever technology to keep us warm and comfortable.

OPEN FIRE

For thousands of years homes had fires that burned wood, coal or peat. Some early homes were built around an open fire pit, which burned day and night. However, these fires needed a lot of work. People had to collect fuel for them and clear away the ash. Fires were also dangerous if not looked after carefully, so someone always had to watch them.

UNDERFLOOR HEATING

In the first century BCE, a Roman engineer named Caius Sergius Orata may have been the first to invent a central heating system known as the hypocaust. This used heat from a single source to warm an entire building. A large fire in one part of the house heated air that flowed through spaces under floors and up walls, warming the rooms from the inside.

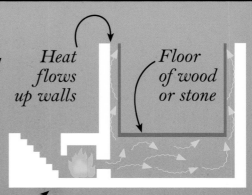

Heat flows up walls

Floor of wood or stone

Heat from a fire warms the spaces beneath the floor.

👉 CENTRAL HEATING

Modern central heating uses electricity or burning gas and oil to heat water. This hot water is pumped around the house to radiators. The heat from the radiators then spreads around rooms in the house, creating flowing hot air called convection currents. This system allows people to control the exact temperature by adjusting thermostats, or remotely using apps on their smartphones.

A modern radiator with a thermostat (top left).

SOLAR POWER 👉

Many modern central heating systems rely on fossil fuels to warm homes. These produce polluting gases that can be harmful to the environment and are not sustainable. Solar panels, on the other hand, collect heat from the Sun and use it to warm a liquid, such as water or oil, flowing through them. The heat in the water or oil is then used to warm radiators inside the home, or heat water for baths and showers, without producing pollution.

Water tanks on a roof are heated by solar panels.

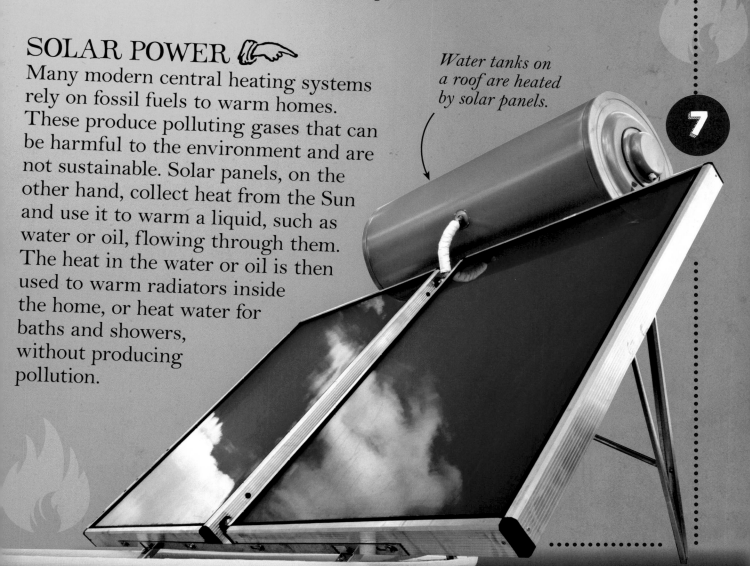

SHINE A LIGHT

At home today, we can flick a switch to turn on a light. However, for thousands of years people relied on fire to see in the dark. Candles and burning lamps are still used in parts of the world where there is no electricity supply.

NAKED FLAMES 👉

Most of the ancient world used simple oil lamps for light. The first use of a candle was by the Romans in about 500 BCE. Roman candles were made of tallow (beef fat). By about 200 BCE the Chinese were using candles made of beeswax. Candles produce little light, so a lot are needed to see, and naked flames indoors were as dangerous in the ancient world as they are today.

A simple pottery oil lamp

👉 GAS LAMPS

Invented at the end of the 1700s, lamps lit by coal-gas were first used to light Europe's factories and streets. Soon, gas was being piped into people's homes, and lit as naked flames. Because the gas was pumped along underground pipes, the lamps didn't need replacing, like candles. However, early gas lamps were dangerous and could explode (left).

☞ GLOWING BEARDS!

The light bulb was developed by several scientists. However, the person credited with the creation of the first successful home light bulb is US inventor Thomas Edison in 1879. The process didn't go smoothly for Edison – he tried more than 1,000 times to get the filament right, even pulling hairs from his assistants' beards to see if hairs would work as filaments. In the end, he found that a bamboo fibre treated with carbon made a long-lasting light filament.

Edison in his famous laboratory at Menlo Park, New Jersey, USA, holding his light bulb

INCANDESCENT LIGHT BULB

An incandescent light bulb works by passing electricity through a tightly wound coil called a filament. As the electricity flows, the filament begins to glow, producing light and heat.

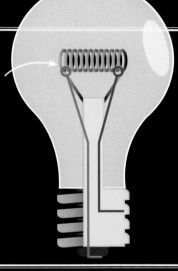

Filament is fixed between two supply wires

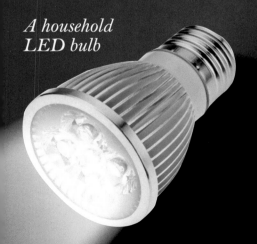

A household LED bulb

☞ ENERGY EFFICIENT

Light-emitting diodes, or LEDs, are more efficient than incandescent light bulbs. They release little heat when they glow and use about one-sixth of the power of a light bulb. They can also last up to 50 times longer. Invented in 1961 by US inventors James Baird and Gary Pittman, LED lights became common in homes only in the 2000s.

STORING FOOD

Food will only stay fresh for so long before bacteria make it unsafe to eat. Over the centuries people have developed many methods of making food last longer, including drying, pickling, smoking and freezing it.

👉📋 PRESERVING

Many ancient food preservation methods are still used today. In hot climates, people preserve food by drying it in the Sun. In cold climates, people store food for the winter by salting (soaking it in salty water), pickling (by keeping it in a liquid, such as vinegar), or smoking it. Smoked food is hung up over a burning fire.

Smoke preserves these mackerel and adds flavour.

Ice brought by ship from the Arctic

KEEP IT COOL 👉

Microscopic bacteria are present in all food, but they slow down their activity if they are kept cold, so keeping food cool helps to make it last longer. In the 1800s, ice was shipped hundreds of kilometres from the Arctic in insulated ships. The ice was then delivered to houses in ice trucks or wagons.

REFRIGERATOR

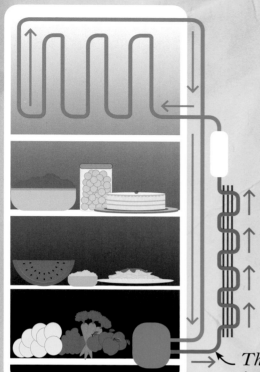

A Scottish inventor, James Harrison, made the first commercial ice-making machine in the mid 1800s. His system is still used in refrigerators today. Pipes circulate a gas called a refrigerant. This enters the fridge through an expansion valve that expands the gas. Since expanding gases cool down, the refrigerant entering the fridge is cold. The cold refrigerant absorbs any heat from inside the fridge and carries it away, making the air inside cooler.

The circulation of refrigerant in a modern refrigerator.

FREEZING FOOD 👉

While on an visit to Labrador, Canada, in 1912–1915, a US scientist named Clarence Birdseye saw how the local Inuit people froze fish in such a way that it still tasted fresh when defrosted. Food-freezing was an old method of preservation, but it was a slow process and it allowed ice crystals to grow in the food, damaging it. Birdseye realised that if food was frozen very quickly, at very low temperatures, fewer ice crystals formed and the food was damaged less. In 1925, he patented a method for flash-freezing cartoned fish on stainless-steel belts. His famous Birds Eye Frozen Food Company was born.

After the Second World War (1939–1945), the only food in plentiful supply in the UK was fish. Clarence Birdseye's frozen fish fingers became very popular.

HOME COOKING

Over the years methods of cooking have changed dramatically, from roaring open fires to sophisticated electric ovens to high-energy radiation that can heat up food in a matter of minutes.

COOKING BY FIRE

The first hearths used for cooking date back more than 250,000 years. These were made by setting rocks on the ground with the fire on top. People roasted meat and vegetables over the flames. The ancient Greeks were the first to build closed ovens made of clay, used for baking bread.

A medieval oven trapped heat inside.

MODERN COOKING

Most home ovens are powered by electricity, which warms an electrical element, or by gas, which burns to heat the oven. The first use of a gas oven was in 1802 by German inventor Zachaus Winzler. Electric ovens appeared in the late 1800s. Fan-assisted ovens, which cook faster by pushing the air around, appeared in the 1960s.

A modern electric oven with compartments for grilling and baking.

☞ COOKING BY SUN POWER

Traditional forms of cooking use fuel, which can create pollution. Solar cookers, however, are low-tech devices that cook food using heat from the Sun. They use shiny mirrored surfaces to collect and concentrate sunlight onto a small cooking area. The best solar cookers can generate temperatures of 550°C. Solar cookers are perfect for remote, sunny regions lacking electricity or gas supplies, and create no pollution at all.

Bread being baked by a solar cooker.

MICROWAVES

Microwave ovens heat food using a high-energy form of radiation, known as microwaves. Inside the oven is a generator called a magnetron. This sends the microwaves into the food compartment. The radiation causes water molecules to jiggle around, heating the food. The heating power of microwaves was discovered by chance in 1945 when US engineer Percy Spencer was working on a radar set, and saw that a bar of chocolate in his pocket had melted. The first food he cooked with microwaves was an egg, which exploded.

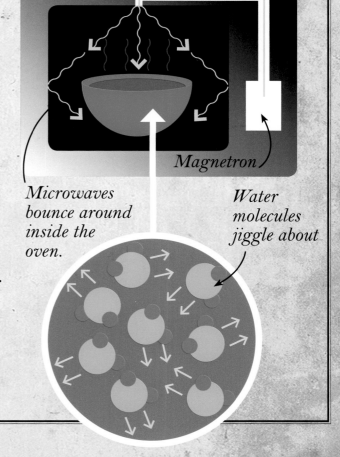

Magnetron

Microwaves bounce around inside the oven.

Water molecules jiggle about

SLEEP TIGHT

The earliest beds were simply straw or furs placed on the floor. This remained the bedding for poor people for centuries. The wealthy slept on mattresses stuffed with feathers and soft pillows.

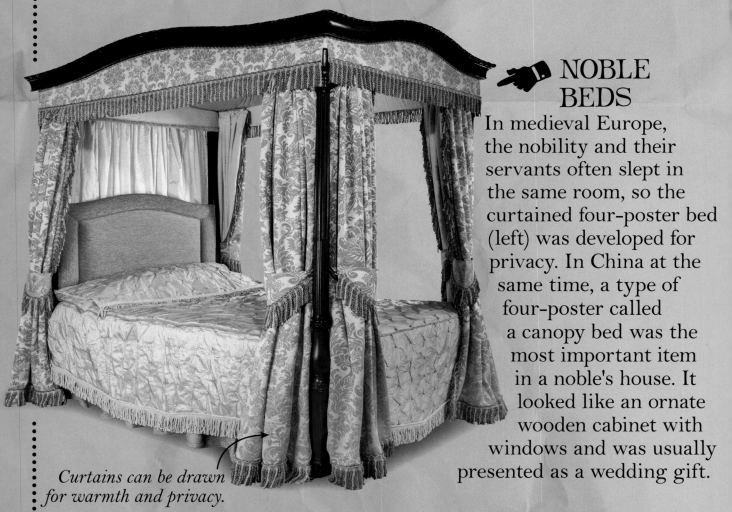

Curtains can be drawn for warmth and privacy.

NOBLE BEDS

In medieval Europe, the nobility and their servants often slept in the same room, so the curtained four-poster bed (left) was developed for privacy. In China at the same time, a type of four-poster called a canopy bed was the most important item in a noble's house. It looked like an ornate wooden cabinet with windows and was usually presented as a wedding gift.

MATTRESSES

Mattresses originated in the Middle East about a thousand years ago as simple thick floor cushions. In 1900, British engineer James Marshall invented a system of wrapped springs to make a mattress bouncy. Some modern mattresses contain a special temperature-sensitive foam that shapes and moulds itself around a body. This 'memory foam' was invented by scientists at NASA in 1966 to make seating safer in aircraft.

A modern memory foam mattress

BEDDING

Ancient Egyptian royalty wouldn't sleep on pillows, but rested their heads on a hard wooden support instead! For centuries, other people tried to get cosy beneath woollen blankets, until the electric blanket was invented in 1912 by US doctor Sidney Russell. Electric blankets are still popular, even though old and faulty ones cause about 5,000 house fires each year in the UK. Today, most of us prefer a nice warm feather duvet.

An Egyptian head rest

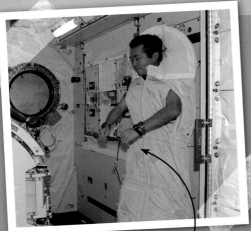

An astronaut sleeps zipped into a sleeping bag.

CRAMPED CONDITIONS

Places where space is tight require different sleeping arrangements. Hammocks provide a quick-to-make bed and have been used on ships for centuries. Because they can swing freely, they also reduce the sensation of the ship rocking. In orbit above Earth, spacecraft have little room, and everything has to be secured to stop it from floating away in zero gravity. Beds on the International Space Station are clipped to the sides of modules.

CLEANING CLOTHES

Cleaning clothes removes dirt and nasty smells. Doing laundry has transformed from being a hard and laborious chore to a task that can be completed with the push of a button.

WATERCOURSES

For thousands of years, people did their laundry on the banks of rivers. Clothes were beaten against rocks and the flowing water washed away the dirt. In some cases, large wooden bats, called washing beetles, were used to beat the dirt out of the fabric. Clothes are still cleaned in this way in many poorer parts of the world.

Laundry washed in a river in Ivory Coast.

A washhouse in San Remo, Italy, in about 1900.

WASHHOUSES

From the early 1800s, people could take their laundry to a purpose-built washhouse, using water from a nearby spring or river channelled into a trough. Washhouses were usually covered to protect people from the weather. They also provided a local point where people could meet, gossip and exchange news.

A hand-cranked washing machine from the 1800s.

👉 WASHING IN THE HOME

In the 1700s and 1800s, new inventions allowed people to clean clothes at home. The mangle used two rollers to squeeze water out of clothes so that they dried faster than clothes wrung by hand. Hand-cranked machines had large drums with paddles that would pummel the clothes to remove the dirt as the drum span. These machines saved time, but using them was heavy work.

WASHING MACHINE 👉

In 1937, the Bendix Corporation of the USA launched the first automatic home washing machine, with a spinning drum powered by electricity. Since then, the machines' design has changed little. Today's machines wash clothes using settings that control temperature. Powerful spin cycles mean that mangles are no longer needed. Some machines also act as tumble driers so that clothes do not need to be hung out to dry.

17

A modern front-loading washing machine.

MODERN MATERIALS

Today, many clothing materials are made from artificial fibres, such as nylon, which was invented by the American Dupont company in 1935. Some artificial fibres do not crease or need ironing. Others are waterproof, breathable fabrics that keep rain out and release vapour from perspiration. Gore-Tex, for example, was invented by US businessman Wilbur Gore in the 1960s. Today, rain jackets and even walking shoes are made of Gore-Tex.

This mountaineer is clad in Gore-Tex.

A beater knocked dust from rugs.

KEEP IT CLEAN

Cleaning a home used to be much harder work than it is today. Dust was swept by hand, and floors had to be scrubbed on hands and knees. Modern technology allows us to clean our homes faster and much more efficiently.

👉 SCRUBBING AND BEATING

Before the invention of vacuum cleaners, scrubbing floors every day could lead to a painful swelling of the knee known as housemaid's knee. Most homes before the 1900s had rugs on wooden floors, rather than fitted carpets. Cleaning rugs was hard, tiring work. They were carried outside, hung up and beaten with carpet beaters to knock the dust and dirt out of them.

EARLY CLEANERS 👉

Vacuum cleaners suck up dust. The first vacuum cleaners appeared in the 1860s and used hand-operated bellows to suck up dust. The first powered vacuum cleaner was created by British engineer Hubert Cecil Booth in 1901. Powered by an petrol engine, it was a huge machine that sat on a cart. Hoses were fed through windows to clean interiors.

One of Booth's original horse-drawn cleaners.

MODERN VACUUM CLEANER

Modern vacuum cleaners are fitted with small electric motors that filter air from dust and suck the dust into a bag. They first appeared in the early 1900s, but they were expensive. After the Second World War, prices dropped as manufacturing techniques became more efficient, making vacuum cleaners very popular. In 1984, British inventor James Dyson created a system that separated dust from air by spinning it very quickly inside the cleaner. This did away with the bags and filters of traditional vacuum cleaners. Dyson created 5,127 prototypes, improving suction and motor power, before finding the right solution.

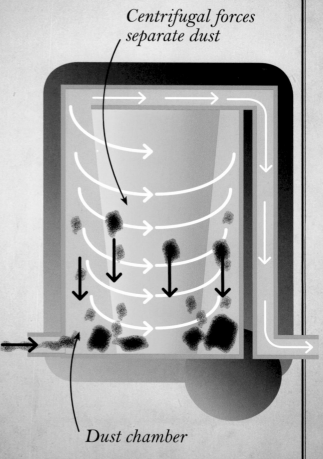

Centrifugal forces separate dust

Dust chamber

ROBOT CLEANERS

Improvements in computer technology have led to the development of automated robot vacuum cleaners. These glide around a room, using sensors to detect and avoid obstructions. They also learn the best route to clean a room, before returning to a re-charging station.

The robot vacuum cleaner uses spinning brushes to sweep up dust.

DOWN
THE PAN

Removing human waste from the home and keeping toilet areas clean is vital for hygiene. Over time, toilets have developed from simple holes in the ground to today's ultra-modern devices.

ANCIENT TOILETS ☞

Several ancient civilisations had toilet systems. The city of Mohenjo-Daro (in present-day Pakistan) was built around 2500 BCE. Its homes had toilets with wooden seats. Waste dropped through holes into street drains. Roman toilets were rows of seats built in bath houses. Waste dropped into a sewer and was flushed away with water.

Roman toilets had no privacy. People chatted as they used them.

☜ HOLE IN THE WALL

The garderobe was a medieval toilet in a castle. It was a room with a hole through which waste dropped into a cesspit. These cesspits needed to be emptied to stop the waste building up too much and this job fell to unlucky people known as gong farmers. They put the waste into barrels, then dumped it on farmers' fields to fertilise them.

← Garderobe

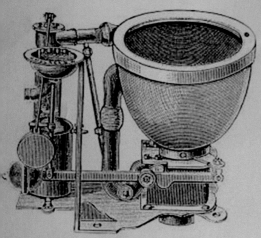

THE FLUSHING TOILET

The flushing toilet was invented by English writer Sir John Harrington in 1596. His device opened a valve to let water out of a tank and into a bowl to flush the waste away. The first practical flushing toilet was built in 1778 by English inventor Joseph Bramah. By the 1800s, many homes had them, especially after Queen Victoria had one installed in the royal bathroom.

Bramah's toilet design of 1778

THE S-BEND

One of the most important developments in toilet design occurred in 1775, when Scottish inventor Alexander Cumming invented the S-bend. This device, still in use today, uses water in the bottom of the bowl to seal the toilet's outlet, stopping unpleasant pongs and whiffs coming up from the sewer.

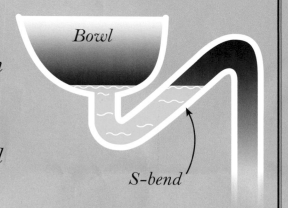

Bowl

S-bend

MODERN TOILETS

Today's toilets have features that make waste removal a more efficient process. These include jets of water around the rim of the bowl to flush waste away, invented by American Philip Haas in 1911, and dual flush systems developed by Australian Bruce Thompson in 1980, which varies the amount of water used in a flush.

This toilet even cleans and dries the user after use.

SAFE AND SOUND

According to the FBI, there are more than eight million property crimes every year in the USA alone. This threat to property has led people to improve security measures to protect their homes, family and belongings.

FORTIFICATIONS

The simplest way to protect your home if you were wealthy was to build it big and strong, with thick walls and strong doors. Early castles had many features to stop people forcing their way in, including high walls and a portcullis (left), which was a large heavy gate that slid down to protect the main door.

LOCK AND KEY

The oldest locks date from Nineveh in ancient Assyria, about 4,000 years ago. Over time, the mechanisms used to work locks have become more complex, making them harder to break open. The Chubb detector lock was made in 1818 by British engineer Jeremiah Chubb. This lock was designed to jam itself locked if someone tried to pick it.

A castle portcullis suspended by chains

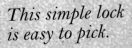

This simple lock is easy to pick.

TUMBLING PINS

Tumbler locks, which are still in use today, use a system of pins of different lengths to lock a door shut. The modern pin-tumbler lock was invented by US locksmith Linus Yale, Jr, in the 1850s. His Yale locks are still made today. They use keys with notches cut out of them. Each notch raises a pin to a set height. If all the pins line up, then the lock's barrel can turn, and the lock opens.

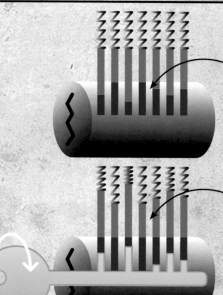

Pins at different heights to close the lock

Pins line up to open the lock

BODY PARTS

If someone stole the key to your house, they could open the lock and steal your things. But what if you were the key? Biometric locks use unique patterns from various body parts to create your very own personal key. These body parts include the unique pattern of blood vessels on the back of your eye (left) and the ridges and swirls of your fingerprints. Today, biometric locks are used to protect homes, safes and even smartphones.

The unique patterns of blood vessels in your eye make a perfect private key.

A finger print scanner reads the swirls and loops of a fingerprint and, if it matches the pattern stored in its memory, opens the door.

SOUND AND VISION

Over the last 100 years, how we listen to music and watch films and television has changed dramatically, from the first crackling broadcasts to today's pin-sharp sounds and images.

The cylinders were played back on a phonograph.

iPod

PLAYING MUSIC

In 1877, Thomas Edison invented the phonograph. This recorded sounds as grooves on a sheet of tinfoil wrapped around a cylinder. Since then, how we play sounds has changed greatly. Vinyl discs appeared in the 1890s and magnetic tape cassettes in 1962 Most recently, the release of digital players, such as the iPod, means that people can carry hours of music in their pocket, or stream songs from the Internet straight to their smartphones.

RADIO

The first commercial radio station began broadcasting in the Netherlands towards the end of 1919. Radio stations soon sprung up all over the world and people could listen to these using radio receivers, which were the size of a cabinet! Over time, improvements in broadcasting technology have seen radio receivers shrink in size. Today you can listen to radio on a smartphone via the Internet (see right).

Early radio set

SENDING SOUNDS AND IMAGES

Radio signal

Sounds and pictures are converted into radio signals, which are sent through the air from a broadcast antenna. These signals are collected by a receiver (either a radio or TV set) and converted back into sounds and images.

Broadcast antenna

Receiver

WATCHING TV 👉

In 1925, British inventor John Logie Baird demonstrated moving television pictures using a device he had built from a tea crate, bicycle light lenses, and sealing wax. It used a rotating disc with holes in it to scan a scene and generate a video signal. From the 1930s, TV sets used cathode ray tubes, which created images with electron beams.

Baird demonstrates a television.

DIGITAL MEDIA

Modern digital broadcasting replaces the traditional analogue radio waves with a digital code. This allows much more information to be sent wirelessly. People can access movies, TV programmes, podcasts and music from the Internet. They can either listen and watch straight away, (this is known as streaming), or download to enjoy whenever they like, using laptops or smartphones.

GAMES

Long before radio and television, people amused themselves at home by playing games. Many of these games are still played. Others are the result of thrilling new technology.

Players who were lucky at Senet were thought to be under the gods' protection.

BOARD GAMES

Games such as chess, a medieval European game, are based on strategy. Others, such as snakes and ladders, on the luck of a dice throw. One of the most famous ancient board games is Senet, a game of chance played by Egyptians more than 5,500 years ago. It involved players moving pieces around a grid of 30 squares. Games also reflect social trends. The hugely popular Cluedo was created in the 1940s in response to a craze for murder mysteries.

MONOPOLY

Monopoly allows players to build a property empire as they move around a board. Created in the 1930s by Charles Darrow, an unemployed US salesman, it was inspired by a game called The Landlord's Game. Darrow started to make sets that had many of the features found on the sets today. Toy companies rejected the game at first because they thought it too complicated. Luckily, they changed their minds and today the game is played in 114 countries in 47 languages.

Women playing
*Blind Man's
Buff in 1804.*

☞ PLAYING IN THE PARLOUR

Parlour games are played by groups, and can involve puzzle-solving word play, guessing answers to questions, or physical activities. In Blind Man's Buff (left), for example, a blindfolded player attempts to find the other players. In charades, players must guess the name of a book or film from acted-out clues.

VIDEO GAMES

By the late 1900s, computer processors allowed games to be played through a games controller. Early computers weren't very powerful. Pong, from 1972, was a crude tennis game. However, improvements in processing power soon led to much faster games with very realistic graphics. These are played on special games consoles, and, if connected to the Internet, allow people on different sides of the world to play each other.

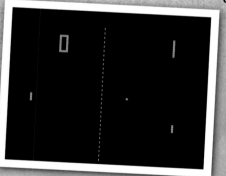

Despite simple graphics, Pong was very popular.

Cameras and sensors in the Xbox kinetic track players' movements and convert them into in-game instructions.

KEEPING IN TOUCH

Before the 1800s, sending a message over a long distance meant dispatching a rider to carry it. The message might take days or weeks to deliver. Today's systems can send images, sound and text at the speed of light.

28

DELIVERING MAIL

The earliest means of message-sending was by runner or horse. In 1860, the Pony Express delivered messages across the USA in just ten days using teams of horses. However, the rides were long and dangerous, and the service only operated for 18 months before it was closed due to competition from the telegraph.

A Pony Express rider sees the building of telegraph poles.

ELECTRIC MESSAGES

The telegraph was a communication system using a network of electric wires. It was invented by British engineers William Fothergill and Charles Wheatstone in 1837. Messages were translated into simple bleeps and spelled out as Morse code.

People took their messages to a telegraph office like this one, for sending in Morse code.

Bell

Handle cranked to generate power.

Receiver

THE TELEPHONE 👉

In 1876, Scottish inventor Alexander Graham Bell built a device for transmitting voices over electrical wires. His 'telephone' revolutionised communication, allowing people to talk to each other even if they were on opposite sides of the world. Bell greeted people on the phone with the word 'Ahoy!'. At first, connections were made by hand by operators at telephone exchanges. The arrival of automatic exchanges meant that calls were connected much quicker. International calls were carried by cables laid across oceans and then through space, with phone signals bouncing off satellites in orbit. Today, we speak on mobile phones and via a network of transmitters.

Bell opens the Chicago to New York telephone line in 1892.

This smart fridge monitors its own contents.

THE INTERNET AGE

Developed in the 1960s as a way for computers to communicate with each other, the Internet has spread around the globe. Today, more than 3 billion people use it to send messages and access information. It allows not only people to communicate but also connected devices to talk to each other. This 'Internet of things' will become increasingly common. Soon, for example, your refrigerator will be able to order food when you're running low, without you needing to shop. Your wrist-worn pedometer may alert your doctor to any health problems.

GLOSSARY

AIR CONDITIONING
The process of changing airflow and temperature for comfort inside a building.

APP
Computer programs designed for use on mobile devices, such as smartphones and tablets.

BACTERIA
Micro-organisms, present in food, that can cause illness if the food is not cooked properly.

CENTRIFUGAL
Moving away from the centre as something rotates.

CESSPIT
A pit for disposing of liquid waste and sewage.

CONSOLE
A set of controls, for example a handset used in computer gaming.

CONVECTION CURRENTS
An air current caused by heated air rising, then cooling and sinking, and then being heated again.

DIGITAL
Electrical technology that operates by code made of the binary digits 0 and 1.

ELECTRICAL ELEMENT
A thin metal device that heats when an electric current is passed through it, such as in an oven.

FABRIC
Cloth made by weaving or knitting.

FILAMENT
A threadlike wire heated to a high temperature by an electrical current so that it glows.

FOSSIL FUEL
Fuels, such as coal, gas, and oil, formed from the decomposition of buried dead organisms.

HEARTH
A brick- or stone-lined fireplace used for heating.

HYPOCAUST
An ancient Roman system of underfloor heating.

INCANDESCENT
Emitting light as a result of being heated.

INSULATED
To protect something from heat loss.

MOLECULE
A group of atoms bonded together.

MORSE CODE
A system of communication using dots and dashes.

PORTCULLIS
A strong, heavy grate that can be lowered to protect a castle gate.

PRESERVATION
In food preparation, a method of keeping food edible for long periods, for example through pickling, smoking or freezing.

PROTOTYPE
An early version of a device, from which others are developed.

RADIATORS
A device for radiating heat.

RECEIVER
A device to receive electromagnetic waves carrying messages or signals.

THERMOSTAT
A device for controlling temperature.

TRANSMITTER
A device to transmit electromagnetic waves carrying messages or signals.

INDEX